THE FLOOD AND NOAH'S ARK

STUDIES IN BIBLICAL ARCHAEOLOGY NO. 1

THE FLOOD AND NOAH'S ARK

ANDRÉ PARROT

Curator-in-Chief of the French National Museums,
Professor at the Ecole du Louvre, Paris,
Director of the Mari Archaeological Expedition

PHILOSOPHICAL LIBRARY

NEW YORK

Translated by Edwin Hudson
from the French

DÉLUGE ET ARCHE DE NOÉ

(Delachaux & Niestlé, Neuchâtel 1953)

Published 1955, by the Philosophical Library, Inc.,
15 East 40th Street, New York, 16, N.Y.

*Printed in Great Britain for Philosophical Library, Inc., by
The Camelot Press Ltd., London and Southampton*

CONTENTS

LIST OF ILLUSTRATIONS

[7]

FOREWORD

For a quarter of a century I have been digging in the Near East—in the land of the Bible. Hence these *Studies in Biblical Archaeology*. Twenty years ago I published a little volume which bore the title *From Babylon to Jericho*, and the sub-title *Does Modern Archaeology Confirm the Bible?* This was in fact no more than a collection of articles that had been written at the request of a small provincial newspaper. To my surprise the first edition sold out in a few days. A second edition was also rapidly exhausted. I did not feel, however, that the book warranted a further edition: it dealt too summarily with too many questions. But I have not repudiated that youthful work, representing as it does an important stage in my career.

The twenty years since then have left their mark in greying hairs, but my enthusiasm remains undimmed, as does my conviction that the believer has nothing to fear and much to learn from the resurrection of the biblical past under the pick of the excavators. The important thing is not to read into the documents what is not there. If one tries to prove too much from them, one finishes up by proving nothing at all, at the same time bringing discredit on a science whose discoveries are imposing enough to do without specious adornment.

It is my intention to deal with certain well defined subjects upon which light is thrown by modern archaeology. I shall try to do so as objectively as possible, for

I am more concerned with producing evidence than with pleading a case. While avoiding all discussion that is too technical for the general reader, I must crave his indulgence where a certain amount of detail is essential. For those who wish to go more deeply into the subject frequent references will be provided.

In inaugurating this series with *The Flood and Noah's Ark* it has been my wish, as well as being topical—a French expedition has lately left for Mount Ararat in search of the Ark—to show not only how Near Eastern archaeology cannot lightly be ignored as one re-reads the story of Noah, but also, and especially, how it has put certain pages of the Book of Genesis in their proper setting and period.

Paris
2nd August 1952

PREFACE TO THE
SECOND EDITION

THE welcome accorded to the *Studies* prompts me to expand the scientific documentation furnished in the first edition. Indeed, several readers, aware of the point of view I represent, have asked for 'more detail'. I accede to this request the more willingly because my purpose remains unchanged. It is to set out the evidences as completely and precisely as possible. Careful documentation is the whole basis of biblical archaeology, and it is essential that those foundations be solid.

20th June 1953

THE FLOOD AND
NOAH'S ARK

THE Flood marks a break in human history. The most diverse traditions look back on the catastrophe as a sort of turning-point; but in my opinion it is advisable to distinguish carefully among all the accounts of it, found all over the world,[1] and to retain here only what relates to the Middle East, or, to be more precise, to ancient Mesopotamia. There can be no doubt that the Flood, which it is proposed to study here from the point of view of its being an historical event, was a *Mesopotamian* disaster.

The inquiry is hedged about with difficulties. It bears upon an event from which we are separated by at the very least five thousand years. Perhaps that is not very long compared with the time that has elapsed since the beginning of the world itself, in the face of the ages which the geologists count in millions of years, or even in comparison with the phases reckoned by anthropologists and prehistorians in tens or hundreds of thousands of years. Archaeologists are more modest, counting themselves very fortunate to have succeeded, in Mesopotamia, in going back to the fourth or the fifth millennium

[1] Some idea of their extent can be gained from reading the pages devoted to it by, among others, Sir James Frazer, *Folk Lore in the Old Testament*, Macmillan, London, 1918, Vol. I, pp. 104–361, and Alfred Jeremias, *The Old Testament in the Light of the Ancient East*, translated by C. L. Beaumont, Williams and Norgate, London, 1911, Vol. I, pp. 245–59.

B.C. Nevertheless even they are conscious of a certain reserve when, from evidence as distant as that, they are asked to form precise conclusions. The field of Middle Eastern archaeology is being widened month by month. That is no cause for regret; let us rather be thankful that it has enabled us to study, in the light of new and indisputable evidence, certain of the biblical narratives, placed henceforth in their correct geographical setting and historical perspective.

1. Tablet XI of the *Epic of Gilgamesh*, containing the account of the Flood. (British Museum)

I

THE FLOOD

1. LITERARY AND EPIGRAPHICAL DOCUMENTATION

The chief account that we have of a flood is in the Old Testament (Gen. 6–8). It follows upon a summary of the lives of the descendants of Adam and Eve. Ten names are recorded in a genealogical table (Gen. 5). Starting with Adam, this list of 'antediluvian' patriarchs ends with Noah, of whom we are told (7.6) that he was 600 years old 'when the flood of waters was upon the earth'.

Exegetical criticism has conclusively demonstrated—and this is admitted by all the experts without exception, Roman Catholic, Protestant and agnostic—that the narrative of Gen. 6–8 is in reality the fusion of two accounts, closely interwoven, one of which (J=Jahvistic) dates from the eighth century B.C., the other (P= Priestly) dating at the earliest from the sixth century B.C.[1]

In order to facilitate comparisons which must be made

[1] De Vaux, *La Genèse*, p. 57: 'This section combines two parallel accounts: a "Jahvistic" account, full of life and colour . . . and a priestly account, more precise and deliberate, but colder. The final editor respected the witness of these two accounts, which tradition had handed down to him, and which are in fundamental agreement. He did not attempt to suppress divergences of detail such as the number of animals taken into the ark . . . and especially the chronology of the flood.' (In this quotation I have omitted the references to the verses attributed to each of the two sources.)

later with extra-biblical literature, I now give in full each of these two versions.

(A) Jahvistic Version

6.5. And the LORD[1] saw that the wickedness of man was great in the earth, and that every imagination of the thoughts of his heart was only evil continually. And it repented the LORD that he had made man on the earth and it grieved him at his heart. And the LORD said, I will destroy man . . . from the face of the ground . . . for it repenteth me that I have made them. But Noah found grace in the eyes of the LORD.

7.1. And the LORD said unto Noah, Come thou and all thy house into the ark; for thee have I seen righteous before me in this generation. Of every clean beast thou shalt take to thee seven and seven, the male and his female; and of the beasts that are not clean two, the male and his female; . . . to keep seed alive upon the face of all the earth. For yet seven days, and I will cause it to rain upon the earth forty days and forty nights; and every living thing that I have made will I destroy from off the face of the ground. And Noah did according unto all that the LORD commanded him. . . .

And Noah went in . . . into the ark, because of the waters of the flood. . . . And it came to pass after the seven days, that the waters of the flood were upon the earth. . . . And the rain was upon the earth forty days and forty nights . . . and the LORD shut him in . . . and the waters increased, and bare up the ark, and it was lift up above the earth . . . all in whose nostrils

[1] *Translator's note:* The English Revised Version, used here, puts LORD in capitals to translate the Hebrew Yahweh.

was the breath of the spirit of life, of all that was in the dry land, died. And every living thing was destroyed which was upon the face of the ground . . . and Noah only was left, and they that were with him in the ark. . . .

8.2. . . . the rain from heaven was restrained; and the waters returned from off the earth continually. . . . And it came to pass at the end of forty days, that Noah opened the window of the ark which he had made: and he sent forth a raven, and it went forth to and fro until the waters were dried up from off the earth. And he sent forth a dove from him, to see if the waters were abated from off the face of the ground; but the dove found no rest for the sole of her foot, and she returned unto him to the ark, for the waters were on the face of the whole earth: and he put forth his hand, and took her, and brought her in unto him into the ark. And he stayed yet other seven days; and again he sent forth the dove out of the ark; and the dove came in to him at eventide; and, lo, in her mouth an olive leaf pluckt off: so Noah knew that the waters were abated from off the earth. And he stayed yet other seven days; and sent forth the dove; and she returned not again to him any more.

. . . Noah removed the covering of the ark, and looked, and, behold, the face of the ground was dried.

. . . Noah builded an altar unto the LORD, and took of every clean beast, and of every clean fowl, and offered burnt offerings on the altar. And the LORD smelled the sweet savour; and the LORD said in his heart, I will not again curse the ground any more for man's sake, for that the imagination of man's heart is evil from his youth; neither will I again smite any more every thing living, as I have done. While the earth remaineth, seedtime and harvest, and cold and heat, and summer and winter, and day and night shall not cease.

The essential substance of this version may be summarized as follows:

1. Yahweh decides to destroy humanity.
2. Yahweh warns Noah of the approaching cataclysm.
3. The flood takes place.
4. Noah learns of the subsiding of the waters through a successive sending out of birds.
5. Noah comes out of the ark and offers a sacrifice of thanksgiving.

It will be seen that J gives no explicit information as to the construction and dimensions of the ark. The priestly version P, on the other hand, which is fond of precision, includes all these details.

(B) Priestly Version

6.9. These are the generations of Noah. Noah was a righteous man, and perfect in his generations: Noah walked with God. And Noah begat three sons, Shem, Ham, and Japheth. And the earth was corrupt before God, and the earth was filled with violence. And God saw the earth, and, behold, it was corrupt; for all flesh had corrupted his way upon the earth.

And God said unto Noah, The end of all flesh is come before me; for the earth is filled with violence through them; and, behold, I will destroy them with the earth. Make thee an ark of gopher wood; rooms[1] shalt thou make in the ark, and shalt pitch it within and without with pitch. And this is how thou shalt make it: the length of the ark three hundred cubits, the breadth of it fifty cubits, and the height of it thirty cubits. A light [R.V. marg.: roof] shalt thou make to the ark . . . and the door of the ark shalt thou set in the side thereof; with lower, second, and third stories shalt thou make it. And I, behold, I do bring the flood of waters upon the earth, to destroy all flesh, wherein is the breath of life, from under heaven; every thing that is in the earth shall die.

But I will establish my covenant with thee: and thou shalt come into the ark, thou, and thy sons, and thy wife, and thy sons' wives with thee. And of every living thing of all flesh, two of every sort shalt thou bring into the ark, to keep them alive with thee; they shall be male and female. Of the fowl after their kind, and of the cattle after their mind, and of every creeping thing of the ground after its kind, two of every sort shall come unto thee, to keep them alive. And take thou unto thee of all food that is eaten, and gather it to thee; and it shall be for food for thee, and for them.

Thus did Noah; according to all that God commanded him, so did he.

7.6 And Noah was six hundred years old when the flood of waters was upon the earth. . . . In the six hundredth year of Noah's life, in the second month,

---

[1] G. H. Gordon, *Introduction to Old Testament Times,* p. 38, proposes to read here *qanim* (reeds) instead of *qinnim* (nests, cells, compartments).

on the seventeenth day of the month, on the same day were all the fountains of the great deep broken up, and the windows of heaven were opened. . . . In the selfsame day entered Noah, and Shem, and Ham, and Japheth, the sons of Noah, and Noah's wife, and the three wives of his sons with them, into the ark; they, and every beast after its kind, and all the cattle after their kind, and every creeping thing that creepeth upon the earth after its kind, and every fowl after its kind, every bird of every sort. And they went in unto Noah into the ark, two and two of all flesh wherein is the breath of life. And they that went in, went in male and female of all flesh, as God had commanded him. . . . And the waters prevailed, and increased greatly upon the earth; and the ark went upon the face of the waters. And the waters prevailed exceedingly upon the earth; and all the high mountains that were under the whole heaven were covered. Fifteen cubits upward did the waters prevail; and the mountains were covered. And all flesh died that moved upon the earth, both fowl, and cattle, and beast, and every creeping thing that creepeth upon the earth, and every man. . . . And the waters prevailed upon the earth an hundred and fifty days.

8.1. And God remembered Noah, and every living thing, and all the cattle that were with him in the ark: and God made a wind to pass over the earth, and the waters assuaged; the fountains also of the deep and the windows of heaven were stopped . . . and after the end of an hundred and fifty days the waters decreased. And the ark rested in the seventh month, on the seventeenth day of the month, upon the mountains of Ararat. And the waters decreased continually until the tenth month: in the tenth month, on the first day of the month, were the tops of the mountains seen. . . . And it came to pass in the six hundred and first year, in the first month, on the first day of the month, the waters were dried up from off the earth. . . . And in the second month, on the seven and twentieth day of the month, was the earth dry. And God spake unto Noah, saying, Go forth of the ark, thou, and thy wife, and thy sons, and thy sons' wives with thee. Bring forth with thee every living thing that is with thee of all flesh, both fowl, and cattle, and every creeping thing that creepeth upon the earth; that they may breed abundantly in the earth, and be fruitful, and multiply upon the earth. And Noah went forth, and his sons, and his wife, and his sons' wives with him: every beast, every creeping thing, and every fowl, whatsoever moveth upon the earth, after their families, went forth out of the ark. . . .

9.1. And God blessed Noah and his sons, and said unto them, Be fruitful, and multiply, and replenish the earth.

The account continues with a reference to the covenant God makes with Noah, setting His bow in the cloud (9.13). Noah, who at the end of the flood was 601 years of age (8.13), had still 350 years to live (9.28). He failed to beat Methuselah, who retained the record for longevity with his 969 years, against the veteran navigator's 950 (9.29).

A comparison of the two versions (J and P) is instructive. Besides the points they have in common, several obvious divergences can be found (the duration of the Flood is given as 40 days in J, and as 150 in P).

The sending out of the birds is not reported in P, nor is the act of thanksgiving, two fundamental features of the Jahvistic account, drawn from an earlier source, as I shall now show.

*   *   *

More important still than the distinguishing of the two accounts in Genesis was the discovery, alongside the biblical version, of an account written in cuneiform script, telling of a Babylonian flood. The circumstances surrounding this find caused such a sensation that it is worth retailing them here.

Following upon the excavations conducted by the British, from 1849 to 1854, on the site of Nineveh, several crates of tablets had been brought to the British Museum. In the store-rooms of the museum lay some 25,000 tablets, not at first very highly prized by the diggers, who, such was the ignorance of all these matters, had taken them to be 'decorated pottery'. Few precautions had been taken; they had been heaped into baskets, loaded on the Tigris, and sent to England. The result was inevitable: the voyage was more disastrous for these documents than had been the taking of Nineveh by the Medes. It was necessary to repair the damage. The curators set about the task, but it proved a long and exacting one, and more than one of them sometimes wondered whether they might not be better employed than in sticking pieces of earth together. True, they were covered with inscriptions, but very few were capable of reading them, much less of understanding them, since the key to the decipherment of Assyro-Babylonian was not found until 1857.

Providentially, the officials were joined in the work by a young and enthusiastic amateur, who rapidly took the lead. George Smith was only twenty-one at the time, and was by profession an engraver of bank-notes. Work of that kind calls for good eyes and clever fingers—two qualities essential for the making of an Assyriologist, who must be able to read and reproduce exactly the most intricate signs. Smith, as well as being an excellent craftsman, was a keen Orientalist. Not only did he spend all his holidays in the galleries of the British Museum, he would often go without his lunch in order to be able to spend more time there, for the museum at that time was open on only three days a week. At the same time he devoured all the books written on the subject by earlier Orientalists.

Birch, the keeper of the Oriental department, noticed this young man with the steel-blue eyes, and, in 1863, took him on as a 'repairer', and gave him the task of piecing together the Nineveh tablets. George Smith brought to the work an intuition that was nothing short of genius, using both colour and shape in matching the tablets. Under his sure fingers the pieces were grouped and classified. The accuracy of his work was checked by the reading of the tablets, for Smith was more than a 'repairer': he deciphered them as well. The work, however, was appreciated only by specialists until, in December 1872, Smith read before the Society of Biblical Archaeology a paper entitled 'The Chaldean Account of the Deluge',[1] and the public at large learned that a cuneiform account of the Flood had been discovered on

[1] Published in the *Transactions of the Society of Biblical Archaeology*, II (1873), pp. 213-34.

a tablet from Nineveh. Public interest was immense, and with one voice scholars demanded that the excavations at Nineveh should be reopened in the hope of finding the missing portions of the mutilated tablet. Furthermore, the proprietors of the *Daily Telegraph* offered Smith a credit of 1,000 guineas to conduct the operation himself, in return for exclusive rights in the reporting of the expedition.

With the consent of the trustees of the British Museum, Smith left for Mosul. In May 1873 he had the extraordinary good fortune to find, after only eight days of searching, a fragment containing seventeen lines, which was not part of the London tablet, but which, by a happy chance, was complementary to it, revealing the contents of the first column which had until then been missing.[1] These first documents on clay and covered with cuneiform writing came from the library of King Assurbanipal (668–26), who had collected in his palace at Nineveh the most valuable copies of works of Mesopotamian literature.[2] The tablets identified in London by Smith belonged to the *Epic of Gilgamesh*, of which they constituted no more than a single episode, recorded on Tablet XI (Pl. I).

THE EPIC OF GILGAMESH

1. *Assyrian Version.* Tablet XI of the Epic of Gilgamesh. Provenance: Nineveh. Contents: 326 lines, of which nearly 200 are devoted to the Flood.

[1] G. Smith's version, *The Chaldean Account of Genesis*, London, 1876, p. 7. It seems that this fragment belongs rather to the Atrahasis cycle (see below, p. 32).

[2] Study No. 3: *Nineveh and the Old Testament.*

The gist of this document is as follows. The king of the
city of Uruk (Erech of Gen. 10.10), Gilgamesh, greatly
affected by the death of his friend Enkidu, has realized
more deeply than heretofore that his life also will some
day come to an end. He recalls that his ancestor Uta-
napishtim (=Uta is my life) was able, alone among all
men, to gain eternal life. He sets out to ask him the
reason for this exceptional lot. Not without difficulty,
he finds him, and asks the immortal to reveal his secret.
The latter, however, does not confide it without hesitation. It is necessary first of all, he says, to obtain from the
depths of the water a plant which restores youth.
Besides this, Uta-napishtim has won immortality only
at the cost of a heroic struggle. What he did was to
survive a flood, whose vicissitudes he relates in these
terms:

Uta-napishtim said to him, to Gilgamesh: 'Gilgamesh, I will reveal unto thee a hidden thing and a
secret of the gods, to thee will I tell it.

'Shuruppak—a city which thou knowest, and which
is situated on the bank of the Euphrates—that city
was already old when their heart prompted the gods
to bring a deluge upon it. The great gods: Anu, their
father; valiant Enlil, their counsellor; Ninurta, their
throne-bearer; Ennugi, who watches over the canals;
Ninigiku-Ea also had sat with them, and their words
he repeated to a reed hut:[1] "Reed hut, reed hut!
Wall, wall! Reed hut, hearken! Wall, attend! Man

[1] Ea employs a subterfuge: he addresses himself to the matting of
which Uta-napishtim's hut is made. The houses (*zarifeh*) of semi-
nomadic Iraqis are still constructed in the same fashion today.
Everything said outside is perfectly audible within.

of Shuruppak, son of Ubar-Tutu, tear down thy house, build a ship, abandon thy goods, seek life! Disregard riches, and save thy life! Take aboard the ship the seed of all life. The ship which thou shalt build, its dimensions shall be measured! Its width and its length shall be equal! On the *apsû*[1] place it!"

'I understood, and I said to divine Ea, my lord: "My lord, what thou hast commanded is a great matter to me, and that will I do. But what shall I answer the city, the people and the elders?" Ea opened his mouth and spoke, he said to me, his servant: "... thou, thus shalt thou speak to them: Verily, me doth Enlil hate, and I may not dwell in your city, nor show my face in the land of Enlil. I will go down therefore to the *apsû* and dwell with my lord Ea. On you will he rain down plenty, the . . . of the birds, the hiding-place of the fishes . . . harvest. [In the morning] it will rain bran (*kukku*), [in the evening], a rain of wheat (*kibâti*)."[2]

'As soon as the first light of dawn shone forth . . . the land was gathered together . . . the . . . brings . . . the . . . brings . . . the men . . . to build it, the child . . . [brought] asphalt, the strong in . . . brought what was needful. On the fifth day, I laid the framework. One *iku*[3] was its surface, its walls were 120 cubits high, and each side of the square roof measured 120 cubits.[4] I set out the shape of its sides and joined them. I

---

[1] *Translator's note:* In Babylonian mythology the *apsû* was a subterranean fresh-water ocean, the abode of Ea, and the source of rivers. Here probably used in reference to the flood-waters.

[2] There is a play on words here: *kukku* and *kibâti*, as well as meaning bran and wheat, are the words for pain and misfortune.

[3] About 4,200 sq. yds.   [4] 120 cubits=65½ yds.

provided the ship with six decks, thus dividing it into seven stories. Within, I divided it into nine sections. Into the midst of it I drove plugs against the water. I chose a boat-hook and stored up what was needful. I poured six *shar* of asphalt into the furnace, three *shar* of asphalt . . . within it. Of the three *shar* of oil the basket-carriers brought, I saved a *shar* of oil which the hold kept in store, two *shar* of oil which the boatman stowed away. Bullocks I slaughtered for the [people], I killed sheep every day. Must, date-wine, oil and wine, I then [gave of it to drink] to the crowd as it were the waters of the river, and [I made] a feast as on New Year's Day. I opened [a pot] of ointment, I laid my hand on it. [On the seventh day] the ship was completed, the . . . were difficult, but the builders loaded the deck of the ship above and below, so that its two-thirds [came under the water].

'[All I had] I loaded aboard her. All I had of silver I loaded aboard her. All I had of gold I loaded aboard her. All I had I [loaded aboard] her. The seed of all life I caused to go up into the ship: all my family and relations. Cattle of the field, wild beasts, craftsmen, I caused them all to go up. The god Shamash had set the time for me: In the morning it will rain bran; in the evening, a rain of wheat, then enter the ship and close thy door. That time arrived: in the morning it rained bran; in the evening, a rain of wheat. Of the day I viewed the aspect: when I beheld the day I was filled with fear. I entered the ship and closed my door. To the pilot of the ship, to the boatman Puzur-Amurri, I entrusted the great structure with what it contained.

'As soon as the first light of dawn shone forth, there came up from the foundation of the heavens a black cloud, and in it roared the god Adad. Shullat and Hanish go before. The throne-bearers go over hill and country. The god Nergal tears out the posts. Ninurta advances, he sets on the attack. The Anunnaki-gods have brought torches, lighting up the land with their flames. The raging of Adad reaches the heavens. All that was bright is turned into darkness. The . . . of the land like. . . . One day the tempest . . . blew fast and . . . the mountain. As soon as the turmoil sweeps down upon [the people] . . . brother no longer sees brother, the people no longer recognize each other.

'In the heavens, the gods were afraid at the deluge and they fled. They ascended to the heaven of Anu. The gods cower like dogs and lie down in the open. The goddess Ishtar cries out like a woman in travail, she cries, the lovely-voiced lady of the gods: "Let this day be turned to clay, when I spoke evil in the assembly of the gods! How have I been able to speak evil in the assembly of the gods, to command a battle to cause my people to perish! I, do I give my people birth so that, like the spawn of fish, they may fill the sea?" The Anunnaki-gods weep with her, the gods howl, they sit down in tears. Their lips are closed, they [await] the end. Six days and [six] nights, strides on the wind, the deluge, the tempest sweeps the land.

'When the seventh day arrived, the tempest, the flood, which had fought like an army, was cowed. The sea rested, the hurricane was silenced, the flood ceased. When I looked upon the sea, all sound was stilled, but all mankind had turned to clay. The plain was become like a flat roof. I opened the window, and the light fell upon my cheek, I fell to the floor and sat down, I wept, my tears ran down over my cheek. I looked at the regions of the sea's horizon. Twelve leagues away . . . there emerged an island. On Mount Nisir, the ship came to rest. Mount Nisir held the ship fast and let it rock no more. One day, a second day, Mount Nisir held the ship fast and let it rock no more. A third day, a fourth day, Mount Nisir held the ship fast and let it rock no more. A fifth day, a sixth day, Mount Nisir held the ship fast and let it rock no more.

'When the seventh day arrived, I put forth a dove and let her go. The dove went and returned; as there was no resting-place for her, she came back. I put forth a swallow and let her go. The swallow went and returned; as there was no resting-place for her, she came back. I put forth a raven and let it go. The raven went, and it saw that the waters were drying up. It ate, it splashed about, it cawed, it did not return. I sent forth everything to the four winds.

'I offered a sacrifice. I placed an offering on the tower of the mountain: I set up seven and seven censers, in their lower parts I spread rush, cedar, and myrtle. The gods smelled the odour, the gods smelled the sweet odour, the gods like flies gathered above the sacrificer.

'As soon as the supreme goddess (i.e., Ishtar) arrives from on high, she brandishes the great fly-whisks (?) which divine Anu had made according to her wish: "O ye gods here present, as truly as I shall

[29]

not forget the lapis lazuli at my neck, I shall remember these days and never forget them. Let the gods approach the offering, but let not Enlil approach the offering, because he did not consider, and brought on the deluge, because he consigned my people to destruction!"

'As soon as Enlil arrived from on high, he saw the ship and was wroth. The god Enlil was filled with fury against the gods, the seven (=Igigi): "Who then has escaped, when no man was to live through the destruction?" Ninurta opened his mouth and spoke, he said to warlike Enlil: "Who but the god Ea can imagine schemes? It is Ea who knows the whole matter." Ea opened his mouth and spoke, he said to warlike Enlil: "O thou, wise among the gods, O warrior, how, how hast thou not considered, and hast brought on the deluge? On the sinner lay his sin; on the transgressor lay his transgression! But loosen a little, that he be not utterly destroyed; forbear, that he be not. . . . Instead of sending a flood, let a lion arise and diminish the people! Instead of sending a flood, let a leopard arise and diminish the people! Instead of sending a flood, let there be a famine and . . . the land! Instead of sending a flood, let the god Irra[1] arise and smite the land! As for me, I did not reveal the secret of the great gods. To the exceedingly wise (*Atrahasis*) I showed dreams, and he heard the secret of the gods. So now his counsel is his counsel."

'Then did divine Enlil go up into the ship, he took my hand and led me away, me he led away, and he

[1] *Translator's note:* Irra was the god of pestilence.

2. The Euphrates below Abu-Kemal

3. The desert after a few hours' rain

caused my wife to kneel at my side. Standing between us he touched our foreheads and blessed us: "Hitherto Uta-napishtim has been a man, but now let Uta-napishtim and his wife be like unto us, the gods! Let Uta-napishtim dwell afar off at the mouth of the rivers!" They took me, and afar off, at the mouth of the rivers they caused me to dwell.'[1]

Such were the theme and the protagonists of the new document. It came, as I have said, from the royal library of Assurbanipal, who, in the seventh century B.C., had had his scribes make copies of the whole of Babylonian religious literature. It would be surprising if it had remained the only one of its kind, and, as digging proceeded, if further copies had not come to light elsewhere. That hope was not to be disappointed. Other tablets referring to the Gilgamesh epic were found at Sippar, Asshur, Uruk, Nippur, Kish, Ur (see map, fig. I) and even in Hittite country. I propose here to do no more than indicate the origin of those tablets which are inscribed with the account of the Flood only.

2. *Babylonian Version.* A badly mutilated fragment, with the elements of thirteen lines, found by Hilprecht. Provenance: Nippur. Date: First Dynasty of Babylon (beginning of the second millennium B.C.). It contains instructions regarding the building of the boat, which is to be a 'racing vessel' (Dhorme), and is to bear the name of 'Preserver of Life'.[2]

[1] *Translator's note:* The translation given here is based on that of E. Dhorme, *Recueil Edouard Dhorme*, pp. 569–79, with slight variations by the present author. For a bibliography, see below, p. 73.

[2] *ATAT*, p. 199; *ANET*, p. 105, X; Heidel, p. 106. I give here only the most recent translations.

The Flood and Noah's Ark

THE EPIC OF ATRAHASIS

As well as the Epic of Gilgamesh, another cycle of legend was known, of which the hero was Atrahasis (the Most Wise). This figure can without hesitation be identified with Uta-napishtim (cf. *Epic of Gilgamesh*, XI, 187). It is therefore not surprising to find in this cycle, of which we are told that the Babylonian text consisted of three tablets, with a total of 1,245 lines, more or less explicit allusions to the Flood. The texts are as follows:

1. *Assyrian Version*. A fragment of seventeen lines, found by George Smith at Nineveh. Often cited as DT, 42. Gives a variant of the conversation between Ea and Uta-napishtim. The hero is here Atrahasis (line 11); he has never built a boat before. The god, Ea, is going to draw for him a plan of it on the ground.[1]

2. *Assyrian Version*. An important fragment, of four columns. Provenance: Nineveh. It appears from this account that Enlil, instead of sending a deluge, had wished to chastise men by subjecting them to a series of plagues. Ea is still the tutelary divinity of Atrahasis.[2]

3. *Babylonian Version*. Provenance: Sippar. A document, unfortunately mutilated, the colophon[3] of which states that it was Tablet II of the series *Enuma ilu awelum* (When a god a man), consisting of 439 lines, copied by a scribe named Ellit-Aya, 'in the year when King Ammi-saduqa rebuilt Dur-Ammi-saduqa, at the mouth of the Euphrates' (i.e. the eleventh year of his

---

[1] *ATAT*, p. 200; *ANET*, p. 105, C; Heidel, p. 110.

[2] *ATAT*, pp. 203–6; *ANET*, pp. 105–6, D; Heidel, pp. 111–16.

[3] The word used to designate the final note inserted at the foot of a cuneiform text.

I. Map of Mesopotamia (places connected with the Flood).

reign, which covered the years 1647–26 B.C.). The narrative told of the presages of the Flood, the threats of Enlil and the favourable intervention of Enki (=Ea), whose protégé is Atramhasis (=Atrahasis).[1]

4. *Babylonian Version*. An important fragment of a badly mutilated tablet.[2] Fifteen lines of column I are fairly well preserved. They contain the instructions given by Ea to Atramhasis, and are in terms identical with those of the Epic of Gilgamesh. At the foot of column 8 the colophon summarizes: 3 tablets, 1,245 lines, by the hand of the scribe Ellit-Aya. The tablet of which we have here a fragment is dated the twelfth year of Ammi-saduqa (a year later than the preceding one). It is thus clear that we possess pieces of Tablets II and III copied by the scribe Ellit-Aya (that found by Scheil, and the other which belonged to A. Boissier), but that nothing so far has been discovered of Tablet I.

THE SUMERIAN VERSION

All the above-mentioned documents are written in Akkadian, a Semitic tongue. They are either copies made in the seventh century B.C. (the Nineveh library), or else tablets written at the beginning of the second millennium B.C. It seemed very probable that these latter tablets were themselves reproductions of still more ancient prototypes of Sumerian origin. This probability became a certainty with the reappearance of Sumerian mythology, a tablet being found which contained a

[1] V. Scheil, *Recueil de travaux*, XX, 1898, p. 55 s.; *ATAT*, pp. 201–2; *ANET*, p. 104, A; Heidel, pp. 107–9.

[2] A. Boissier, *Fragment de la légende de 'Atram-Hasis'*, in *RA*, 1931, pp. 91–7; *ANET*, p. 109, B; Heidel, p. 109.

Sumerian version of the Flood.[1] The details of the document are as follows:

A tablet from Nippur. Intact, it contained at least 300 lines. The beginning (thirty-seven lines) is missing. A god announces his intention to save humanity from destruction. Men may therefore continue to build cities and temples. The work of creation proceeds. (Break of some thirty-seven lines.) Kingship has descended from heaven, and five cities (Eridu, Badtibira, Larak, Sippar and Shuruppak) are founded. (Break of some thirty-seven lines which must have told of the decision taken in favour of sending the Flood.) When the story is taken up again, we find that several divinities (Inanna, Enki) have not approved of the action about to be taken against mankind:

> ... Then wept Nintu like ...
> Holy Inanna [composed] a lamentation for the people of the land.
> Enki called on his own heart's counsel,
> Anu, Enlil, Enki (and) Ninhursag ...
> The gods of heaven and earth [called upon] the names of Anu and of Enlil.
> Then did Ziusudra, the king, the *pashishu* [of] ...
> Build a mighty ...
> Obeying in humility and reverence, [he] ...
> Daily at his task, constantly [he] ...
> Visited by all manner of dreams [he] ...
> Invoking the name of heaven (and) of earth, [he] ...

[1] A. Poebel, in *PBS*, V (1914), No. 1; *PBS*, IV, 1, pp. 9–70; *ATAT*, pp. 198–9; *ANET*, pp. 42–4; Heidel, pp. 102–5.

. . . the gods, a wall . . .

Ziusudra, beside it, stood and hearkened.

'Stand on my left by the wall . . .

By the wall will I speak a word to thee, [hearken to my speech]

[Give] ear to my commandment:

By our . . . a flood [shall invade] the places of worship,

To destroy the seed of mankind . . .

This is the decision, the decree of the assembly [of the gods].

By the command of Anu (and) of Enlil . . .

Their kingship, their dominion [shall be abolished].'

(Break of about forty lines.)

The hurricanes, in monstrous fury, attacked as one;

At the same time the deluge swept over the places of worship.

Then, for seven days (and) seven nights,

The flood was poured out over the land,

(And) the great ship was tossed by the hurricanes upon the mighty waters.

Utu came forth, he who sheds light over heaven and earth.

Ziusudra opened a window in the great ship;

Utu, the hero, cast his beams into the interior of the giant boat.

Ziusudra, the king,

Fell on his face before Utu.

The king kills an ox, slaughters a sheep.

(Break of about thirty-nine lines.)

[36]

'Thou shalt send forth a "heavenly breath", an "earthly breath", in very truth, he shall stretch himself out by your . . .[1]

Anu and Enlil sent forth a 'heavenly breath', an 'earthly breath', by their . . . he stretched himself out.

Vegetation arose from the bosom of the earth.

Ziusudra, the king,

Fell on his face before Anu and Enlil.

Anu (and) Enlil cherished Ziusudra,

They give him a life like that of a god,

The breath of eternal life, like that of a god, from on high they bring him.

Then Ziusudra, the king,

The preserver of the name of vegetation (and) of the seed of mankind,

In the land of the crossing, the land of Dilmun, the place where the sun rises, they caused him to dwell.

(*The remainder of the tablet, some thirty-nine lines, has been destroyed.*)

BEROSUS' ACCOUNT

The last extra-biblical narrative relating to the Flood that must be mentioned is that given by Berosus, a priest of Marduk, writing in Babylon about the year 275 B.C. Unfortunately this work has not survived, and we know it only from extracts collected by the Greek historian

[1] The text is extremely difficult here. One translator, S. N. Kramer, writes: 'Lines 251–3, although fully preserved, are at present extremely difficult to render, and the present translation is to be considered as highly doubtful.' *ANET*, p. 44, note 56.

Alexander Polyhistor (first century B.C.), a native of Miletus. These extracts were used by Eusebius of Caesarea (A.D. 267–340) in his *Chronica*; but once again they are known to us only through a further intermediary, Syncellus (ninth century of our era)! A complete Armenian recension makes it possible to check and, if need be, rectify the Greek text. In spite of a transmission spread over more than a thousand years, the account is not without interest. It runs as follows:

'After the death of Ardates, his son Xisuthros succeeded, and reigned eighteen sari. In his time happened the great deluge, the history of which is given in this manner. Cronus appeared to him in a vision, and gave him notice that upon the fifteenth day of the month Daisios there would be a deluge, by which mankind would be destroyed. He therefore enjoined him to bury all the writings containing the history of the beginning, procedure, and final conclusion of all things, down to the present term; and to leave them in the city of the Sun at Sippar; and to build a vessel, and to take with him into it his friends and relations; and to convey on board everything necessary to sustain life, and to take in also all species of animals, that either fly or rove upon the earth; and when all was prepared, to trust himself to the deep. If he were asked whither he wished to sail, he was to reply, "To the gods, in order to plead with them for the good of mankind." And he obeyed the divine admonition: and built a vessel five stadia in length, and in breadth two. Into this he put everything which he had got ready; and last of all conveyed into it his wife, children, and friends.

'After the flood had been upon the earth, and was in time abated, Xisuthros sent out some birds from the vessel; which not finding any food, nor any place to rest their feet, returned to him again. After an interval of some days, he sent them forth a second time, and they now returned with their feet tinged with mud. He made a trial a third time with these birds, but they returned to him no more: from whence he formed a judgement, that the surface of the earth was now above the waters. Having therefore made an opening in the vessel, and finding upon looking out, that the vessel was driven to the side of a mountain, he immediately quitted it, being attended by his wife, his daughter, and the pilot. Xisuthros immediately kissed the earth: and having constructed an altar, offered sacrifices to the gods. These things being duly performed, both Xisuthros and those who came out of the vessel with him, became invisible. They who remained in the vessel, finding that the others did not return, came out and sought them, and called continually on the name of Xisuthros. Him they saw no more; but they could distinguish his voice in the air, and could hear him admonish them to pay due regard to the gods; and likewise inform them that it was on account of his piety that he was translated to live with the gods; and that his wife and daughter, with the pilot, had obtained the same honour. To this he added that he would have them return to Babylon, and, as had been told them, to search for the writings at Sippar, which were to be made known to all mankind: and that the place where they then were was the land of Armenia.

The remainder having heard these words, offered sacrifices to the gods, and journeyed on foot towards Babylonia.

'The vessel being thus stranded in Armenia, some part of it yet remains in the Kurdish mountains in Armenia; and the people scrape off the bitumen, and carry it away, and make use of it by way of an alexipharmic and amulet. In this manner they returned to Babylon; and having found the writings at Sippar, they set about building cities, and erecting temples: and Babylon was thus inhabited again.'[1]

It is not possible for me to give here in detail the cuneiform sources of Berosus' narrative, to indicate the points in common, or to note where the traditions differ, and where the latest in date is burdened with folklore. I must however remark upon the notable fidelity shown in the proper names: *Ardates* is transcribed in the Armenian text as *Otiartes*, employed for *Opartes*, formed from *Ubar-Tutu* (Epic of Gilgamesh, XI, 23, and W.B.444, 62; see below, p. 41), the father of the Mesopotamian survivor of the Flood. In the name *Xisuthros*, given by Berosus, is easily seen the *Ziusudra* of the Sumerian epic. The reference to *Sippar*, the city of Shamash, the deified sun, is also not surprising, when one remembers the intervention of Utu, designated by name in the Sumerian text (see above, p. 36). It is clear that the Babylonian priest was not only drawing upon a good source, but also relying for his narrative upon the most ancient documentation then known, that of the Sumerians.

[1] *Translator's note:* I have followed in the main the translation given in I. P. Cory, *The Ancient Fragments*, 1828, where the Greek text is also to be found.

The Flood

Apart from these detailed narratives, it should be pointed out that the catastrophe of the Flood is also explicitly mentioned in certain documents of a historical nature, one of which has been known for only twenty-five years. There is, firstly, the prism acquired by an English collector, Weld-Blundell, and usually referred to by Assyriologists by its catalogue number, W.B.444.[1] This text is an enumeration of the kings who reigned in Babylonia from the origins down to the end of the Dynasty of Isin (2022–1797 B.C.). It is completed by another tablet belonging to the same collector and bearing the number W.B.62.[2] Although much shorter—it consists of only eighteen lines—it is of great importance for us, since on it appear the names of the antediluvian kings. We ought not, of course, to accept without reserve the information it gives, particularly as to the number of years covered by the various reigns, but it is interesting to find reappearing on these lists names of individuals known from the epic narratives.

Thus, the prism W.B.444, after enumerating the five antediluvian cities (Eridu, Badtibira, Larak, Sippar and Shuruppak), gives the name of the king of Shuruppak: Ubar-Tutu. We have already seen that this is precisely

[1] This text has been published by S. Langdon, in *Oxford Editions of Cuneiform Texts*, University of Oxford—Ashmolean Museum, 1923, II, Bk I–IV, pp. 8–21. See the study on it by Dhorme, 'L'aurore de l'histoire babylonienne', *Recueil Ed. Dhorme*, pp. 3–79, and the important monograph by T. Jacobsen, *The Sumerian King List*, Oriental Institute of the University of Chicago, 1939.

[2] Published by Langdon, in *Journal of the Royal Asiatic Society*, 1923, p. 256.

the name given by the Epic of Gilgamesh as that of the father of Uta-napishtim.

On the tablet W.B.62, two kings of Shuruppak are given: Su-kur-lam, son of Ubar-Tutu, and Ziusudra, son of Su-kur-lam. Here, then, are the protagonists of the Sumerian account of the Flood (Ubar-Tutu and Ziusudra), with, in addition, one Sukurlam, who may well be a fictitious personage.

After the mention of Ubar-Tutu and the recapitulatory note (5 cities, 8 kings, 241,200 years), we read on W.B.444: 'The Flood came. After the Flood had come, kingship descended from heaven. The kingship was at Kish.' Then follows the list of postdiluvian cities and dynasties.

*　　　*　　　*

There can, then, be no question that the Flood marked a clear break in history. The memory of it remained vividly in men's minds as well in Mesopotamia as in Palestine, where Jesus made reference to it during His last days of preaching (Matt. 24.37–9; Luke 17.26–7).

To sum up, we have at our disposal in biblical and in Babylonian literature a collection of texts referring to a devastating cataclysm from which one family escaped, thanks to an 'ark': the family of Noah, according to the Bible, that of Uta-napishtim, Atrahasis, Ziusudra or Xisuthros, according to the Babylonians. The relationship of all these stories is undeniable; it is apparent at once to the least practised eye. One might construct a synopsis of them, with variations, of course, but in their essentials showing impressive agreement. Let me indicate some of the most striking parallels:

The Flood

GENESIS	CUNEIFORM TRADITION
Yahweh decides to destroy humanity because of man's wickedness.	The gods decide to destroy humanity because of the error of its ways.
Yahweh warns Noah and tells him to build a boat.	Ea (Enki) warns Uta-napishtim (Ziusudra) and tells him to build a boat.
This boat is to be filled with animals, so that their kind shall be preserved on all the earth.	This boat is to be filled with animals and with the seed of all life.
The Flood comes. Yahweh has blotted out all the beings who were on the face of the ground.	The Flood comes. All humanity has returned to clay.
Noah learns of the subsidence of the waters by sending out birds (raven, dove).	Uta-napishtim learns of the subsidence of the waters by sending out birds (dove, swallow, raven).
Noah builds an altar and offers a sacrifice to Yahweh.	Uta-napishtim offers a sacrifice to the gods.
Yahweh smells the sweet savour.	The gods smell the pleasant odour.
Yahweh ceases from cursing men (version J).	Enlil is reconciled with Uta-napishtim.
Yahweh blesses Noah and his sons (version P).	Enlil blesses Uta-napishtim and his wife.

*   *   *

Which is the narrative that forms the basis of all the others? The answer ought to be: that which is the oldest; and the oldest is clearly the Babylonian narrative. Such an answer frightens certain biblical scholars, who propose a middle-of-the-way solution which is in their eyes less dangerous to the doctrine of inspiration. Originally, they say, there was a primitive tradition (as yet undiscovered), of which we possess two versions, the

[43]

Sumero-Babylonian on the one hand, and the Israelite on the other.[1] I frankly confess that I find this theory scarcely satisfactory. I prefer to consider that in and with the biblical narrative of the Flood we have the Israelite version of a Mesopotamian tradition[2]—of which the originals on clay tablets are in our possession —revised by the biblical narrators in the light of monotheism, without their having always troubled to eliminate certain quite realistic anthropomorphic features,[3] features which need in no way shock us, now that we understand them in the light of the history of religion. If now I am asked how it is that this Mesopotamian tradition turns up among the spiritual writings of Israel, I shall simply reply that the tradition of the Flood was brought—along with most of the traditions recorded in the first eleven chapters of Genesis—by the patriarchs who emigrated from the Land of the Two Rivers and settled in the land of Canaan. The Israelites never tried to conceal the fact that their ancestors had at that time 'served other gods' (Josh. 24.2), that is shared beliefs quite foreign to the Jahvistic faith. That is why we have in Chapters 6 to 8 of Genesis the account of the Flood which the Mesopotamians set down in cuneiform, long before the Jahvistic authors thought of putting it into

[1] This theory is expounded by Hillion, *Le déluge dans la Bible et les inscriptions sumériennes et akkadiennes*.

[2] A thesis put forward by J. Plessis, 'Babylone et la Bible', in *Dictionnaire de la Bible*, but with exegetical concepts (the two parallel accounts, J and P, taken by Moses and incorporated by him almost without alteration in Genesis) which are questionable, to say the least.

[3] In the Jahvistic account (the older of the two, see above, p. 16) Yahweh *closed* the ark behind Noah (Gen. 7.16), and, again, He '*smelled* the sweet savour' of the sacrifice (Gen. 8.21).

writing. With extraordinary fidelity the oral tradition in Israel had preserved the moving story over a period of one thousand years.[1]

*   *   *

2. ARCHAEOLOGICAL DOCUMENTATION

We come now to the second aspect of the question. We have seen that the Bible and Babylonian literature have witnessed literally and historically to the fact of the catastrophe of the Flood. Is it confirmed by archaeological evidence?

It seems probable, *a priori*, that a disaster whose magnitude cannot be in doubt must have left traces in the soil of Mesopotamia. One ought to find there the thick deposits of alluvium which would be left by the unleashing of great masses of water. Granted the antiquity of the event, which must be at least prior to the year 2000 B.C. (the oldest narrative, the Sumerian, must go back to that date), such traces would be found only at a considerable depth, that is to say *beneath* recent historical strata, which the pick finds almost at the surface. Every stratigraphical excavation was thus susceptible of yielding valuable information in this

[1] I place the patriarchal migration in the eighteenth century B.C.; and the Jahvistic school, according to biblical scholars, is situated in the eighth century B.C. It should be pointed out that certain characteristic details, such as the successive sending out of birds, would seem to give the J version in Genesis (eighth century) priority over the Assyrian version of the Epic of Gilgamesh (seventh century). But we must not be deceived by this, for it seems almost certain that we are not yet in possession of the *Babylonian* original, preserving the same characteristic detail, since it has been proved that the Epic of Gilgamesh (*Assyrian* version) was preceded, as I indicated earlier, by two older versions, one *Babylonian*, the other *Sumerian*.

respect. For once, too, excavators, who like to discover 'objects', would have cause to rejoice if they found none, for alluvial deposits usually contain no traces of human activity. How great would the temptation be to see in such a 'sterile' stratum evidence of the flood of which

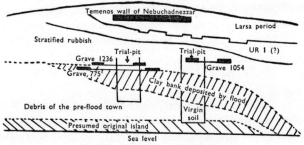

II. Ur: Stratigraphical section.

literature speaks! At least two excavators have succumbed to that temptation: both Sir Leonard Woolley and Stephen Langdon affirmed unhesitatingly that they had discovered the traces and the material proofs of the Flood, the former on his site at Ur, the latter at Kish. What ought we to think of this?

In the course of his campaign of 1928–9, Woolley, making a stratigraphical section (fig. II), reached a layer of 'clean water-laid clay' whose thickness varied from 3.70 m. to 2.70 m.[1] Above it the 'purely Sumerian' civilization was to be found, while beneath it lay a 'mixed culture', characterized by painted pottery. Woolley, in fact, did somewhat modify his assertions, recognizing that the lower culture had not been entirely submerged. Of this culture there remained painted

[1] *Antiquaries Journal*, IX, October 1929, p. 329.

4. Sacred boat, Uruk cylinder (*c.* 3000 B.C.). (After A. Moortgat, *Vorderasiatische Rollsiegel*, Pl. 6, No. 30)

pottery and some odd figurines in the shape of naked women with snake-like faces and wigs of bitumen, some of them bearing a child in their arms.[1] The excavator, nevertheless, concluded that this alluvial layer had been deposited about the middle of the fourth millennium by an inundation which was indeed 'the Flood of Sumerian history and legend, the Flood on which is based the story of Noah'.[2]

Shortly afterwards, Langdon announced amid great publicity (*Times, Daily Telegraph, Illustrated London News*) that he also had found, at Kish—this time, therefore, in the region of Babylon—the material traces of the Flood. In the face of such assurance it is understandable that even specialists were at first carried away, and that an Orientalist as experienced as M. Dhorme was able to write, upon this double announcement being made: 'It is now certain that the date put forward by Langdon for the cataclysm (3300 B.C.) can be adapted to the Ur discoveries as well as to those at Kish.'[3] Woolley, on the other hand, finding that the honour of making this sensational discovery was no longer exclusively his, lost no time in contesting Langdon's dates. 'In order to avoid a confusion already prevalent,' he wrote,[4] 'I must refer to the discovery of a diluvial deposit at Kish, which also has been held to represent the Flood of Sumerian legend.' This deposit, he declared, was certainly not the same as that at Ur. The dates advanced were incorrect,

[1] *Antiquaries Journal*, X, October 1930, pp. 329–41.

[2] L. Woolley, *Ur of the Chaldees*, Ernest Benn, London, second edition, 1950, p. 29; *Excavations at Ur*, Ernest Benn, London, 1954, pp. 34–6.

[3] *Revue Biblique*, 1930, p. 484; and *Recueil Edouard Dhorme*, p. 564.

[4] *Antiquaries Journal*, X, October 1930, p. 340.

and the Ur deposit was the true Flood. This controversy, and the great difficulties involved, did not deter enthusiasts such as Sir Charles Marston, who calmly

Surface

Neo-Babylonian

Babylon I

Agade

Red stratum

Flood deposit 4

Cemetery Y — Flood deposit 3 / Flood deposit 2 / Flood deposit 1

Water table

Virgin soil

III. Kish: Stratigraphical section.

records that the two scientists had simultaneously discovered the sedimentary deposits left by the great Flood.[1]

The matter is by no means so easily settled. It requires

[1] Sir Charles Marston, *The Bible is True*, Eyre and Spottiswoode, London, 1934, p. 67.

above all a more careful examination of the observations made on the Mesopotamian sites. At Ur, the flood deposit intervenes in the course of the protohistoric Obeid period, characterized among other things by painted pottery and figurines, and situated chronologically in the fourth millennium. At Kish, C. Watelin, who directed the excavations, adopted a much more cautious position than Langdon. One has only to read his report to realize that there is a considerable divergence of views between the two men.[1]

Above the cemetery Y (fig. III) was found a sedimentary deposit 30 cm. thick, corresponding to a serious inundation (in addition, three other minor inundations had preceded it), but it seems impossible that this can represent the Flood of literary tradition.

Watelin's reasons for this conclusion are essentially these: Gilgamesh, who learned of the deluge from the mouth of Uta-napishtim, must have lived *after* that event. However, there were found *below* the flood layer some cylinder impressions actually representing Gilgamesh. He would in that case have lived *before* the Flood, which is impossible. In any case, Watelin concludes, the flood deposit of Ur and that of Kish do not correspond (fig. V). They testify to different inundations, provoked no doubt by torrential rains and not, as has been maintained, by a tidal wave. According to the Watelin-Langdon chronology, the date of the Kish flood layer is 3000 B.C. Actually it must be put at least two centuries later.

[1] Watelin and Langdon, *Excavations at Kish*, University of Oxford, IV, pp. 40–4, p. 53 (stratigraphical section), and Pl. I (objects found above and below the flood deposit).

Let us look now at other sites. At Uruk, between the archaeological layers I and II, Jordan[1] records a sterile stratum, five feet in depth, which V. Christian[2] has no hesitation in interpreting as the mark of a heavy inundation. Stratigraphically, this deposit would go back to the beginning of the third millennium, layer II marking the end of the protohistoric Jamdat Nasr period, which ended about the year 2800 B.C.

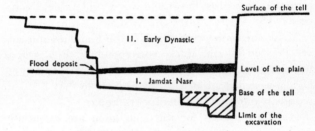

IV. Fara: Stratigraphical section.

A similar layer has been found at Fara (the Shuruppak of literary tradition, home of the Mesopotamian hero Ziusudra-Uta-napishtim). An alluvial stratum some 2 ft. thick separates the Jamdat Nasr (I) and Early Dynastic (II) levels[3] (fig. IV).

I must recall here that at Tello (the ancient Lagash), in the course of the 1930–1 campaign, working on *tell* K, I myself had to remove a sterile layer before reaching the Jamdat Nasr period. I did not feel justified in recognizing it as a flood deposit, for it was more like a

[1] J. Jordan, *Zweiter vorläufiger Bericht* . . . , Abhandlungen der Preussischen Akademie der Wissenschaften, 1929, p. 20.

[2] V. Christian, in *Archiv für Orientforschung*, VIII, p. 64.

[3] E. Schmidt, 'Excavations at Fara', in *Museum Journal*, XXII, 1931, pp. 201, 217.

sub-foundation of packed soil prepared for subsequent building than a sedimentary deposit. I described it as the 'foundation soil' of one of the temples of Lagash.[1]

One further discovery which may have a bearing on the Flood is that made at Nineveh. In their great stratigraphical section,[2] more than 100 ft. deep, R. C. Thompson and M. E. L. Mallowan noted between 60 ft. and 54 ft. a layer which they describe as follows: 'Consecutive series of thirteen strata: mud and riverine sand alternating, the accumulation of a well-defined pluvial period indicating an important climatic change.' The two excavators put forward no interpretation, contenting themselves with speaking of a 'pluvial interval'. As for its chronological situation, between the 'prehistoric' periods I and II of Nineveh (=Halaf and Uruk periods), this puts it in the fourth millennium, clearly in the Obeid era—i.e. it corresponds with the Ur deposit.

What conclusions are we to draw from these observations? Without adopting the negative theses of certain writers,[3] I think that the following can be admitted: on several Mesopotamian sites, sedimentary strata have been recorded (fig. V). These strata seem to represent deposits left by more or less violent overflowings of either one or both Mesopotamian rivers. It should be noted that archaeology has furnished the evidence not of one inundation but of several (it is not in fact possible to place in the same period the Ur flood deposit and those of Kish, Uruk, or Shuruppak). I believe that one

[1] A. Parrot, *Tello*, Albin Michel, Paris, 1948, p. 58.

[2] *Annals of Archaeology and Anthropology*, XX, p. 134 and Pl. LXXIII; *ILN*, 16 July 1932, p. 98.

[3] J. Bright holds that Mesopotamian archaeology has furnished 'no trace of Noah's Flood', *The Biblical Archaeologist*, V, 1942, p. 58.

of these cataclysms was accompanied by destruction on such a scale, and made such an impression, that it became one of the themes of cuneiform literature. This was *the* Flood, of which legend has no doubt exaggerated the violence and the destruction, whereas archaeology indicates that not all the cities suffered equally.

PERIODS	DATES	UR	KISH	SHURUPPAK	URUK	LAGASH	NINIVEH
EARLY DYNASTIC	2470 2800						
JAMDAT NASR	2800 3000						
URUK	IVth MILLENNIUM						
OBEID							
HALAF							

V. Mesopotamian sites showing flood deposits.

I believe also that this inundation was occasioned primarily by more than usually violent flooding of the Euphrates (Plate 2) and the Tigris, which could easily sweep away human habitations in an area that is quite flat. The destructive action of the flooding was probably increased by torrential rains—a Westerner can have no idea of the intensity of which they are capable (Plate 3)—the memory of which has been preserved in the biblical tradition, whether it speaks of forty days of rain (Gen. 7.4, 12 [version J]), or of the windows of heaven being opened (7.11 [version P]).

A tidal wave has also been suggested. In spite of

certain objections,[1] the possibility cannot be ruled out, and the breaking-up of the 'foundations of the great deep' (Gen. 7.11) might be a reference to the sudden onrush of the waters from below joining the waters from above to bring about annihilation. Yet some human beings escaped annihilation: those who took refuge in the ark.

[1] According to Watelin, *Kish*, IV, p. 43, analysis of the sedimentary deposits at Kish and Ur revealed no trace of sea shells or of marine animals.

II

THE ARK

What was the ark like? Insofar as archaic drawings can be interpreted, we find that the Babylonians constructed their boats in various ways.

Often they contented themselves with a sort of raft made of bundles of reeds laid together and bound at intervals with several thicknesses of cord (fig. VI *a*). Sometimes they used round creels (fig. VI *b*), that is to say enormous baskets of woven osiers coated with pitch and bitumen to make them watertight. Such vessels may still be seen today on the Tigris at Baghdad, where they are used as ferries. A third type was the *kelek*, a sort of raft made buoyant by means of inflated skins (fig. VI *c*). The Assyrians were expert in the art of manœuvring them, and Victor Place, in 1855, used them to transport the great bas-reliefs found by him at Khorsabad.

Finally, there was a type of boat very often found engraved on cylinders, which resembled the modern *belem*, with its flat bottom and its high prow and stern (fig. VII).

The boat immortalized by the Flood story was of dimensions so imposing that, frankly, they are hard to imagine, for they present problems of construction which those who are not too concerned with precise accuracy will prefer to pass over in silence.

The Sumerian text is too defective to give any information on this subject. According to the Babylonian version (the Hilprecht fragment, see above, p. 31), it was to be a 'large vessel' (*eleppu rabitu*) of a special type (*eleppu qurqurru*: 'racing vessel', Dhorme; 'giant boat', Heidel; 'ark', Speiser). Owing to the mutilated state of the cuneiform documents, the dimensions have been preserved only in Tablet XI of the *Epic of Gilgamesh*.

The first indication given (line 30) is that the length and breadth were to be equal. This somewhat unexpected piece of information must have seemed incorrect to Berosus, who gives a ratio of 5:2 between the length and breadth.[1] The cuneiform tablet continues: *one iku* (about 4,200 sq. yds.) *was its surface, its walls were 120 cubits* (65 yds.) *high, and each side of the square roof measured 120 cubits* (lines 57–8). It would follow that Uta-napishtim's boat was shaped exactly like a cube, and was therefore much more like a box than a ship. It was divided horizontally by six floors, which, counting the ground floor, gave it seven stories. Each of these decks was in turn divided into nine sections (lines 60–2), giving a total of 63 compartments. There follow details of the loading. Thus weighed down the boat floated with two-thirds of its height under water (line 79).

What does the Book of Genesis say? The Jahvistic account (see above, p. 16) is silent on the point: it is not interested in dates and dimensions. On the other hand, the Priestly account (P) is more precise: 300 cubits long, 50 wide, and 30 high—i.e. roughly 166 yds. × 28

[1] Berosus gives the following figures: length 5 stadia (1,010 yds.), breadth 2 stadia (404 yds.). The Armenian recension indicates even higher figures, devoid of any possible verisimilitude: length 15 stadia (3,030 yds.)!

yds. × 17 yds. One also finds mention of the stories, reduced to three (Gen. 6.16), and of the rooms (the Hebrew word is *qinnim*) (6.14), facilitating the separation of the different species of animals. The use of pitch is attested both by the Epic of Gilgamesh (XI, 65–6) and by the Bible (Gen. 6.14).

Comparing the two documentary sources, the data given by the Bible are much nearer modern ideas of shipbuilding, for the description of the Babylonian vessel makes it much more of a coffer than a boat. No doubt it would float, but it would be far less suitable for anything like real navigation, in spite of the fact that reference is made to a pilot for it, one Puzur-Amurri (XI, 94). At any rate, in each case we have a construction of considerable size. It is a pity that we do not possess any valid iconographical evidence of it.

All the representations we possess are in fact of smaller boats, none of which could rival the 'large vessel' of Uta-napishtim or the ark of Noah. With its length of 166 yds. the Patriarch's boat would bear comparison with many modern liners displacing up to 15,000 tons—indeed, it would be nearly half the length of such vessels as the Cunarders *Queen Mary* and *Queen Elizabeth*. We do not know how long it took to build. The Priestly account (P) notes at one point that Noah was 500 years old when he begat Shem, Ham and Japheth (5.32), and at another that he was 600 when the Flood came (7.6). Some people have concluded from this that the Patriarch took a hundred years to build his boat! I can find no support in the texts for such a deduction, particularly as we ought not to forget either that at that period in the history of the human race all the ancients

a

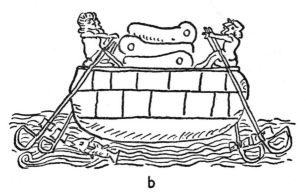

b

c

VI. Ancient Mesopotamian navigation: (a) Raft of reeds;
(b) Creel; (c) Kelek.

seem to have had notions about figures different from our own.

*   *   *

That being all the information we have, it is not at all easy to form a clear idea of the boat which victoriously braved the waters of the Deluge. Illustrators and carvers, however, have never been put off by that: the Flood and Noah's ark are among the biblical themes most often depicted. It would be pleasant to choose and describe the most original representations. I believe the oldest would be those in the Catacombs of Rome (second century A.D.), on Christian tombs, and the next in a mosaic in the synagogue of Gerasa (fifth century A.D.), but the monument is so badly mutilated that apart from the names of Shem and Japheth hardly anything is left but the symbolical dove perched on a tree and holding a branch in her beak.

On the other hand the ark is intact in the extraordinary cycle of paintings at St. Savin (eleventh-twelfth centuries), and the vessel, tossed by the waves that engulf mankind, advances majestically with its figurehead in the form of a mastiff's head, and its monumental three-storied superstructure, in which may be discerned, dominating the various kinds of animals, the four couples (Noah and his wife, and his three sons with their wives) calmly surveying the scene. The same delightful realism is to be seen in some of the Romanesque capitals: those, for instance, of the Collegiate Church of Beaune, or of Autun Cathedral (twelfth century); and also in the mosaics of the Apocalypse at St. Sever (twelfth century).

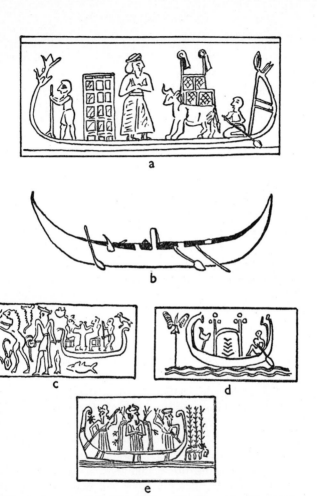

VII. *Ancient vessels:* (*a*) *Uruk;* (*b*) *Ur;* (*c*) *Shuruppak;*
(*d*) *Lagash;* (*e*) *Louvre cylinder A, 157.*

The tradition, once started, never ceased being exploited in accordance with the genius or the personality of the artists concerned. Raphael used it when he was working in the *Stanze* in the Vatican, as did Michelangelo when he decorated the Sistine Chapel. After them the theme also appears in Titian and Carracci. Commissioned by Richelieu to paint pictures representing the Four Seasons, Poussin took four stories from the Old Testament to symbolize them: the Garden of Eden for Spring, Ruth and Boaz for Summer, the cluster of grapes from the Promised Land for Autumn, and the Flood to represent Winter. Nature is destined to be destroyed; the serpent, the cause of the disaster, is sliding over a rock; but on the waves there rides the Ark, the affirmation of hope.

Although many artists have dwelt on the dramatic aspect of the story (it is no more than we should expect in Romantics such as Girodet, Géricault or Gustave Doré), others, as numerous, have recalled the deliverance, and, in particular, the moment when the ark, come to rest on the mountain-side, is about to open to permit the survivors to offer the sacrifice of thanksgiving. Michelangelo, while capable of depicting the anguish of the old man lifting up the body of his drowned son, or of the mother fleeing with her peacefully sleeping child, was also able to turn from those dramatic scenes to depict the burnt-offering, whose victims await only the lighting of the fire which is to consume them. It is the final act, the act of reconciliation, with the ark amid the clouds. The survivors are taking up their life again, abandoning the ark of their salvation. It is the moment for us to ask what became of that ark,

since again and again men have set out in search
of it.

*   *   *

The Epic of Gilgamesh (XI, 138–44), the reader will
remember, gives the exact spot where Uta-napishtim's
boat came to rest once more on the ground: 'I looked
at the regions of the sea's horizon. Twelve leagues away
there emerged an island. On Mount Nisir the ship came
to rest. Mount Nisir held the ship fast and let it rock no
more. One day, a second day, Mount Nisir held the
ship fast and let it rock no more. A third day, a fourth
day, Mount Nisir held the ship fast and let it rock no
more. A fifth day, a sixth day, Mount Nisir held the
ship fast and let it rock no more. When the seventh day
arrived, I put forth a dove. . . .' Mount Nisir may be
situated between the Tigris and the Little Zab.

The Jahvistic account gives no information on the
point. Version P states that 'the ark rested in the seventh
month, on the seventeenth day of the month, upon the
mountains of Ararat' (Gen. 8.4). As always in the Old
Testament, Ararat is the name of a country (II Kings
19.37, R.V.; Isa. 37.38, R.V.; Jer. 51.27), quite certainly to be identified with the *Urartu* of the Assyrian
inscriptions, which corresponds to the modern Armenia.
Berosus, as we have seen above (p. 40), had also been
acquainted with a tradition according to which Xisuthros' vessel had grounded on 'the Kurdish mountains
in Armenia'. It seems to me that Berosus was attempting
thus to reconcile two different traditions, the one which
spoke of Urartu (Armenia) and that which referred to
Kurdistan (Mount Nisir). In any case a discrepancy

exists between the Epic of Gilgamesh on the one hand and the biblical version P on the other. It seems that as time went on there was a tendency to put the resting-place ever farther to the north of Mesopotamia, in the district where the highest mountains were known to be; that is, the mountains which must have been the first to re-emerge as the waters subsided. Henceforth we are well on along the road of folklore and marvel, and moving farther and farther away from history.

Berosus had echoed the tradition of the Kurdish mountains. We find it again in Josephus (*Antiquities*, I, 3, 6), but here also is the fuller version given by Nicolaus of Damascus: 'There is above Minyas in Armenia a great mountain called Baris, to which, as the story goes, many people fled for refuge in the flood and were saved; they say too that a certain man, floating in an ark, grounded on the summit, and that remains of the timbers were preserved for a long time.'[1]

An Arabic manuscript in the library of the Convent of St. Catherine on Mount Sinai preserves the allocation of living-space inside the ark: beasts and cattle in the hold, birds on No. 2 deck, and human beings on the top deck, women on one side and men on the other, with the corpse of Adam, exhumed for the occasion, forming a barrier between them in the middle.[2]

The Mount Ararat tradition, however, is contested by Musulmans and Syrians, who point to Mount Judi, which is considerably further south, and from which the plain of Mesopotamia can be seen. This rival mountain will have its place in the final episode, being played out in our own day: the Invention of the Ark.

[1] Frazer, *op. cit.*, I, p. 110.   [2] Frazer, *op. cit.*, I, pp. 145–6.

THE INVENTION OF THE ARK

People do look for the ark, and from time to time they find it. It goes on drawing men like a magnet—men, that is, who do not discriminate clearly between legend and fact. About 100 years ago the following paragraph appeared in a periodical:

'From the time of the Flood up to the nineteenth century, no one has dared to undertake the ascent of the sacred mountain. The Armenians were opposed to any such attempt with a religious prejudice that had the force of a dogma. They believed and still believe now that Noah's ark had remained intact on the summit, and that in order to preserve it from destruction God had forbidden anyone to go near it. This belief rests on a legend about a monk, a relative and contemporary of St. Gregory, who had had the pious wish to go up to the summit, but had been stopped on the way by God Himself. A deep sleep kept falling upon him, during which he redescended all the distance he had just laboriously climbed; and at last, pitying his fruitless efforts, God sent an angel who told him as he slept that the top of the mountain was inaccessible, but that as a reward for his labours God would send him a fragment of the ark which rested there. This fragment is still preserved today as the most precious relic in the cathedral of the monastery of Echmiadzin, the seat of the Armenian Patriarch' (*L'Univers illustré*, No. 281, Thursday 1 October 1864).

That the ascent of Ararat (16,945 ft.) was no easy matter seems certain. The mountain remained un-climbed for a long time, until it was at last conquered in 1829 by a namesake of mine, G. F. Parrot, a climber already famous for his ascents in the Alps (Monte Rosa)

and the Pyrenees (Mont Perdu).¹ It was again climbed
in 1850 by a topographical expedition under Colonel
Khoelzko. In 1876, Lord Bryce, on a trip to the Ararat
range, found on a rocky slope at an altitude of over
13,000 ft. a piece of wood which he humorously identified
as a spar from the timber of the ark.² After Lord Bryce,
amateurs desisted from the enterprise until in 1916,
during the First World War, a Russian airman named
W. Roskovitsky, flying over Mount Ararat, declared
that he had observed on one of the slopes of the mountain
the remains of an ancient vessel. The Czar at once
organized an expedition, which, we are told, found the
remains in question and brought back a description of
them which was conclusive as regards their identification.
It is most unfortunate that no competent person saw this
report, which was lost during the course of the Bolshevist
revolution of 1917. All we have is Roskovitsky's story,
of which the least that can be said is that if it is shorn of
reminiscences of Genesis, scarcely anything is left.³

That did not prevent several American periodicals⁴

¹ Account of the ascent of Ararat in Zurcher and Margollé, *Les
ascensions célèbres aux plus hautes montagnes du globe*, p. 137. I am in-
debted for this reference to M. R. Boigeol.

² Quoted by Frazer, *op. cit.*, I, p. 109, n. 2.

³ The account was published in 1949 by the *Journal de Genève* and
reproduced by *Ecclesia*, November 1949, pp. 45–6, which gives it
'rather as a curiosity than as a certainty'. *Noir et blanc* (23rd July
1952) takes it up again without reservation under the title: 'Noah's
Ark Discovered and Visited.' So is History written.

⁴ According to *The Biblical Archaeologist*, V (1942), p. 59, these
were: *Defender of the Faith*, October 1942; *The King's Herald*, November 1941; *Prophecy*, March 1942. Two of them published retrac-
tions afterwards. These periodicals had in fact been preceded by the
Kölnische Illustrierte Zeitung, which had, on 1 April 1933, announced
the discovery of Noah's Ark on Mount Ararat. However, I have it
from Pastor C. Berron, of Reitwiller (Bas-Rhin), that this was an
April Fools' Day joke.

from proclaiming the sensational news. Serious specialist organs reserved for it the fate it deserved: silence. *The Biblical Archaeologist*, observing that the whole story was without foundation, dismissed it in one line: 'It may be regarded as a symptom of man's willingness to believe what he wishes to believe.'

But such cautionary episodes go unheeded. During the summer of 1949 the popular press and radio announced the departure of an American expedition, directed by Dr. Smith, a retired missionary from North Carolina, accompanied by W. Wood (an engineer), E. J. Newton (a decorator), and W. Ogg (a physician). The mission was rewarded with complete failure, reported not without humour by the French newspapers.[1]

Meanwhile the affair had been further complicated. Headlines in a Parisian newspaper[2] announced: 'WE HAVE SEEN NOAH'S ARK . . . BUT NOT ON MOUNT ARARAT. Two Turkish journalists have discovered on Mount Judi, on the Mesopotamian border, a vessel 500 ft. long.' It makes pleasant reading, for everything one could wish for is there. The journalists saw everything, that is to say that they were shown everything they wanted to see: the imposing remains of a vessel 500 ft. long, 80 ft. wide and 50 ft. high, some bones of marine animals, and, a few miles away, Noah's tomb itself!

[1] A few of the headlines: 'No ark in sight', 'Noah's Ark not at the rendez-vous' (*Combat*), 'Explorers give up search for Noah's Ark' (*Figaro*). *Le Monde* (24 September 1949) reports gravely: 'So much for Dr. Smith's divine revelation, for he claims to have had a celestial communication ordering him to pack his trunk and go in search of the remains of the Ark.' The same paper also tells us that 'the funds necessary for such an expedition were easily found, since certain enthusiasts had no hesitation in selling their peaceful businesses in order to join the explorers'.

[2] *France-Soir*, 31 August 1949.

I do not intend to present my readers with a critical study of this story, seething as it is with contradictions, the most flagrant of which is this: at first, the journalists report that they have seen with their own eyes the remains of the ark. They finish up by invoking the testimony of ancestors who used to tell of seeing the ark appearing from time to time like a ghost ship under its covering of mud. It transpires then that in 1949 there was nothing at all to be seen. Anyhow it does not matter very much, since here we are with two arks to choose from: one on Mount Ararat and one on Mount Judi, both of them attributed to Noah. The reader will agree with me that, whatever the circumstances, that is one too many. I am reminded of Jerusalem, where often the Latins and the Orthodox Greeks will show you holy places consecrated to the same event, yet distinct and distant the one from the other. At Jerusalem, one says to oneself in such circumstances: it is either one or the other. With the Ark, whether on Ararat or on Judi, we need have no hesitation: neither one nor the other!

M. J. de Riquer, a former member of French polar expeditions, does not share my scepticism. With M. F. Navarra he left France in June 1952 at the head of an expedition which included a number of associates, and two cine-photographers.[1] It was preceded to Turkey

[1] As soon as M. de Riquer's project was announced (*Libération*, 25 October 1951), I made my own views known (*Carrefour*, 31 October 1951). In an interview with a reporter of *Samedi-Soir* (17 November 1951) Professor Massignon declared: 'Of course he has no chance of finding the Ark, even if it ever existed. But one must not discourage a man of good will. It would not be the first time that, starting from a false premise, someone had made a totally unexpected discovery.' M. Dupont-Sommer (ibid.) suggested the possibility that travellers had noticed, and airmen flown above, some commemorative monument or chapel set up 'towards the end of the Middle

by the Abbé Pierre, himself a Turk, with 'a good know-
ledge of the regions through which the expedition would
have to pass'. One more attempt to be added to the file—
not so much of archaeology as of mountaineering, and,
as far as the latter goes, a very fine effort.[1]

Ages, for example,' by 'a group of anchorites or monks' to recall
the 'miraculous adventure of Noah in the actual surroundings in
which biblical tradition holds that the Patriarch and his family
touched dry land'. Several newspapers reported the departure of
the expedition: *Le Monde*, 6 June 1952; *Relais*, 27 June 1952, with
a portrait over an ambiguous caption which does not make it clear
whether it refers to M. Riquer or to an actor in the film 'L'aventure
sans retour' ('The Adventure without Return')! The title was, to
say the least, not happily chosen. Finally, *Noir et blanc* (23 July
1952) devoted a double page to the expedition, with pictures which
include one of the cars about to leave Paris, bearing a placard:
'Mount Ararat Expedition', and another photograph with the
legend: 'On the road to Mount Ararat, donkey-drivers make way
for the cars of the French expedition.' Film-producers make a habit
of taking their shots of the Sahara on the artillery-range at Vin-
cennes. Perhaps, too, 'the road to Mount Ararat' passes through
Morocco or Algeria. . . .

[1] The mountaineering was successful: 'The Turkish flag was
hoisted on the highest point of the mountain' (*Le Monde*, 19
August 1952), but 'Noah's Ark was not found on Mount Ararat'
(*Le Monde*, 10 September 1952). 'INTROVABILE L'ARCA DI NOÈ'',
read a headline in an Italian paper. Undiscovered—and for a very
good reason!

III

THE RELIGIOUS ASPECT
OF THE FLOOD

We have come to the end of our study, but I think that
it is only right to add a few words on the religious aspect
of the event. That the cuneiform tradition and the
Biblical accounts are related is undeniable. But their
obvious similarities should not prevent us from recognizing that in religious inspiration they are radically
different. Two scholars such as Father de Vaux and my
own teacher Adolphe Lods are at one in bringing out the
contrast between the rude and fantastic polytheism of
the Babylonian deities, and the sovereign majesty of the
one God who, although He has decided to destroy sin-
ners, has none the less separated out the righteous Noah
in order to save him. It is, however, not absolutely
correct to say that the idea of his righteousness saving a
man from punishment is absent from the Babylonian
tradition. We have seen (p. 30) that when Enlil sees the
boat and the survivors, and flies into a rage, Ea speaks
in defence of Uta-napishtim, and, though admitting
that the sinner should be punished for his sin, the
transgressor chastised for his transgression, he asks for
mercy: 'Loosen a little, that he be not utterly destroyed'
(Epic, XI, 181). Similarly, in the plea which he addresses
to the god of the earth he puts forward clearly the

[68]

principle of the punishment being proportionate to the gravity of the offence. Before sending the flood, he declares, Enlil ought first to have used a more limited chastisement, calling upon a lion, a wolf, famine or pestilence as the agent of execution (Epic. XI, 182–5).[1]

Again, one of the most moving parts of the Mesopotamian legend is that where Enlil pardons his creatures, taking them by the hand: 'he took my hand and led me away, me he led away, and he caused my wife to kneel at my side. Standing between us he touched our foreheads and blessed us: "Hitherto Uta-napishtim has been a man, but now let Uta-napishtim and his wife be like unto us, the gods!"' (Epic, XI, 190–4). That benediction is echoed by God's blessing given to Noah and his sons, thanks to which they will be able to be fruitful, multiply, and replenish the earth (Gen. 9.1, 7, version P), but for them there is to be no earthly immortality—that had been finally lost at the Fall.

We know how the Fathers of the Church enlarged upon the story. The author of the First Epistle of Peter had shown the way, when he wrote (3.20–1) that the water of the Flood had prefigured the water of Christian baptism. It is a slippery road, and there are many who, following the example of the Early Fathers, continue to venture upon it. For the record I shall give only one example of typological interpretation. Turning over the pages of 'the late Monsieur le Maistre de Sacy's *History of the Old and New Testaments with Edifying Examples,* in honour of Mgr. le Dauphin' (Paris, 1713), I was struck

[1] Dhorme puts forward an interesting comparison with the plagues sent by Yahweh against a guilty land: famine, wild beasts, sword and pestilence (Ezek. 14.13, 15, 17, 19, 21) (*Recueil Edouard Dhorme,* p. 597).

by the composure with which the author put forward exact dates. In the year of the world 1536 (i.e. 2468 B.C.), God had spoken to Noah, giving him complete instructions for building his ark. The vessel was ready when, in the year of the world 1656 (i.e. 2348 B.C.) the flood came.[1] And here is the 'edifying explanation':

'The Holy Fathers have observed that this ark was visibly the figure of the Church, which is the sole Ark in which a man may find salvation, and without which he is lost eternally. The mighty size of this construction which was borne upon the water, and this assembly of all manner of clean and unclean beasts, represented the extent of the Church throughout all the earth, and the calling of many nations and peoples differing among themselves in the diversity of their habits and customs, whom God, whose will it is that all men should be saved, would one day join together in this refuge, in order that they might find a like salvation and escape a like shipwreck.

'The wood and the water visibly represent two great mysteries: the water, that Baptism which washes us clean of sin, as the Flood purified the world of its abominations; and the wood of the Cross of the Saviour, who has saved the whole world, and who is still today the only hope of Christian folk, who look for salvation only through its infinite cost. Thus did it please God to

[1] The Maistre de Sacy was not alone in proposing exact dates. *Le Véritable Messager boiteux de Montbéliard* (a provincial almanack) for 1803, put the creation of the world in the year 5752 B.C., and the 'universal deluge' in 4095 B.C. The Comtesse de Ségur, in the *Bible d'une grand-mère* (Hachette, 1878), placed the Flood in 2348 B.C. Especially delicious is the conversation (pp. 34–5) between grandmother and grandchildren on the subject of the building of Noah's Ark.

prefigure His Church in that Ark, which served for the mending and renewing of the world. And we ought always to render to God our thanks that He has brought us into it, to save us from the Flood of sin and transgressions which inundates the whole earth. Some few things there may still give us cause for apprehension: we may suffer offences and ills there, as the Holy Fathers have observed; within the Ark troubles may occur, but there is no salvation to be found elsewhere; and who is not safe within it will undoubtedly perish in the Flood.'

To this 'explanation' there is nothing that can be added. Every interpretation that is sincerely made is legitimate and worthy of respect. Whether it is truly in harmony with reality and with the simplicity of the facts is another matter. In these *Studies* it is those facts alone which concern us, and I shall do my best to avoid mixing dogmatics with archaeology. There is, however, one moral which I may be permitted to point.

The biblical narrative and the cuneiform tablets have all omitted entirely to tell us what happened to the ark. Let us therefore imitate their discretion and accept not knowing *whither* we may turn or *what* we may handle. Faith is not dependent on such perishable relics—and besides, I imagine that after five thousand years the wood of the ark, even coated with pitch, has long since returned to dust. It is then surely a waste of time to set out in search of it—especially since, even without an ark, we still have the promise made to Noah: 'While the earth remaineth, seedtime and harvest, and cold and heat, and summer and winter, and day and night shall not cease' (Gen. 8.22).

How great a blessing that is can be judged from the

fact that since the days of Noah men have desired no other. One would like to be sure that men will always be wise enough not to disturb with the inventions of their hands that equilibrium of life which results from Nature's contrasts. Remember the gods of the Assyrian tablet, fleeing in terror up to the heaven of Anu, powerless to stop the awful cataclysm which they had let loose. The rhythm of the seasons—or sorcerer's apprentices: that, finally, is the alternative; such is the lesson that is to be learned from our long contemplation of the Ark.

BIBLIOGRAPHY

I give here only those works in which are to be found the most recent editions or translations of texts relating to the Flood.

The text of the Epic of Gilgamesh has been published by R. Campbell Thompson, *The Epic of Gilgamish* (1930). There are numerous translations: in English, R. Campbell Thompson *The Epic of Gilgamish* (1928); E. W. Budge and C. J. Gadd, *The Babylonian Story of the Deluge and the Epic of Gilgamesh* (British Museum, 1929); A. Heidel, *The Gilgamesh Epic and Old Testament Parallels* (1949), pp. 16–101; E. Speiser in J. B. Pritchard, *Ancient Near Eastern Texts relating to the Old Testament* (Princeton University Press, Princeton, 1950), pp. 73–99 (I refer to this in the notes as *ANET*); in French, Dhorme, *Choix de textes religieux assyro-babyloniens* (Paris, 1907); G. Contenau, *L'épopée de Gilgamesh* (1939) and Tablet XI, in *Le déluge babylonien* (1952); in German, Ebeling, in H. Gressmann, *Altorientalische Texte zum Alten Testament* (1926), pp. 150–98 (referred to in the notes as *ATAT*); A. Schott, *Das Gilgamesh-Epos* (1934); in Dutch, F. M. Th. Böhl, *Het Gilgamesj-Epos* (1941); second edition, revised (1952). An interesting study on the subject of the ark: Edward Ullendorf, 'The Consecration of Noah's Ark', in *Vetus Testamentum*, IV (Leyden, 1954), pp. 95–6. 'Discoveries at Ur', in Sir Leonard

Woolley, *Excavations at Ur* (London, 1954, Ernest Benn), pp. 19–36.

For the Epic of Gilgamesh and the Flood-story see also C. Virolleaud, *Légendes de Babylone et de Canaan* (1949), and the study by J. Plessis, 'Babylone et la Bible', in *Dictionnaire de la Bible, Supplément*, by L. Pirot (1928).

INDEX